Table of Contents

For Abigail and Zachary

Introduction

It was my first night home from hospital, and I'd just woken from a strange nightmare. It was the same one I'd had three years earlier, and once again I felt an immense sense of loss.

Where was my baby?

Half-awake, half-asleep, I frantically began searching the bed. As my hand brushed against my no-longer-pregnant belly, panic set in. I pulled the covers off the bed and ripped away the sheets, desperate to find my baby.

Once I was fully awake, lying in a pool of sweat with heart palpitating, I realised I'd given birth some days ago and my second baby was sound asleep in the crib next to me.

This nightmare, like the one I'd suffered three years earlier after having my first child, was a stark reminder. Because despite all the joys, highs and immense pleasure of becoming a parent, I had an overwhelming feeling that I'd lost more than just the pregnant belly.

I also felt incredibly inadequate. "Wow, you've only been home from hospital for one night and you've *already* misplaced the baby!" And this was on top of the pressure I'd already put on myself to do this mothering gig the "right" way.

But it wasn't long before this strange nightmare became the start of a dream.

As my journey into parenthood took shape, I started thinking how I could make the transition into parenthood easier for others. Antenatal classes tend to gloss over the emotional aspects of parenting, even though it's probably the toughest thing to deal with after labour.

Suddenly I saw a gap I desperately wanted to fill. And as a medical practitioner, perinatal educator and mother of two young children, I felt confident that I could do it.

Having run workshops on "Emotional Preparation for Parenthood," I know what a privilege and responsibility it is to educate parents on what this massive transition might *feel* like. And so began my mission: to reassure and prepare other parents for the transition, while respecting the fact it will be different for everyone.

Some experts say women don't want to hear about emotional issues or the challenges that may lie ahead, and want to focus on preparing for labour and birth. Other experts say women *do* want to hear it, but in a dedicated forum and perhaps when they are less focussed on the birth.

I believe there's an element of denial when it comes to emotions, especially challenging ones. Women don't want any grey clouds or bubbles being burst during their time of joy (and it *is* a joyful time).

This book isn't about bursting your bubble. Instead it offers support to launch yourself *out* of the bubble and beyond, and guidance to become a more self-aware parent.

A recent study in Melbourne, Australia showed that parents who were given information and support to help them prepare for the challenges of a new baby were more likely to seek help, felt more competent and had less depression than those without the information and support.*

I've written this book to fill a void: preparing parents for the emotional challenges of parenthood. I know it exists because I get the same response from *every* mum when I tell them about my workshop and book: "Ooh, I wish I had you in the early days of having a new baby."

I've spent the past few years connecting with parents who generously and kindly opened their hearts and shared their experiences and transition journeys. And I've shared a lot of their stories in this book, because it's all part of moving from person to parent.

This isn't a parenting book. It holds no promises or black and white answers. And you won't find anything about labour, breastfeeding or the physical care of mum and baby either. Instead it's a guide for you and your partner to make the transition from person to parent with confidence and emotional wellness.

Good luck!

* http://www.jad-journal.com/article/S0165-0327%2810%2900674-9/abstract

Realistic expectations

Despite everything you've read, seen and been told about becoming a parent, often it feels as if nothing can prepare you for the reality. One way to get through it is to keep your expectations as realistic as possible. This chapter explores some of the ways to keep your head above water when real life with a baby isn't what you imagined it would be.

The reality of being a parent may be different from what you expected.

A question many new mums and dads often ask is, "Why didn't anyone tell me it would be like this?"

(I've asked myself the same question. Many, many times.)

As a first-time parent it can be hard to imagine what your life will be like until you're living it, complete with babe in arms.

Annette, a business owner and mother of two young boys, resented things not being as she imagined they'd be:

> It took me the birth of my two children (plus more time), to eventually learn to *"expect the unexpected"*.

> It is natural to imagine how you would *like* your birth experience to be, and how you picture yourself in your new parenting role. However, all too often the real life experience does not match your initial expectations.

> There is nothing that can prepare you emotionally and physically for every possible birth or parenting scenario.

> The only thing that you can prepare yourself for, is to "expected the unexpected" and know, *you **can** and **will** deal* with whatever situation and experience arises, despite how difficult it sometimes feels.

> *I expected a full term baby*, but instead I got a premature one. We had to commute to and from the hospital several times a day for a few weeks. What a shock that was.

I expected to breast feed my baby, but instead my baby did not develop his sucking reflex so for hours each day I had a machine attached to my breasts and extracted milk (I felt like a cow), so I could feed my own milk to my baby through his naso-gastric tube. Then, for months after, I kept filling up bottles with breast milk to feed him. I never expected to feel so physically and mentally wrecked. Some days it felt like my brain did not function. When I look back I wonder how I ever did it. *But you just do.*

I expected to sit at my computer every day when my baby slept so I could continue to develop my business, but instead, I got a baby who never slept and my computer never got switched on. Sometimes I got so frustrated and felt resentful toward my baby for prohibiting me from doing what I wanted to do. It took me over two years to finally stop expecting to achieve in my work, and just be with what I was blessed with.

I expected a healthy baby, but instead I got a baby that was intolerant to almost everything he ate, not to mention the many ambulance rides we experienced when he hardly could breathe! Nothing can prepare you for that.

I expected to be a calm and grounded mother, but often I found myself (and still do) losing patience and feeling like I wanted to run away from parenting! There were times I developed terrible bouts of anxiety.

Now, five years after the birth of my first child, I have two very healthy, strong boys who sleep, eat, play and bring us so much joy, laughter and tears!

Most new parents don't expect resentment, anxiety or stress and tension to get mixed in with their joy. But it's a common feeling, and perfectly normal. After all, your life has changed forever. Who wouldn't feel resentful when life has changed in so many ways?

By giving yourself permission to grieve what you've lost, you'll be able to move forward.

Coming to terms with the reality of parenthood may be challenging.

It's easy to warn new parents how they'll need to be flexible. They all seem to realise life with a new baby is often chaotic and lots of hard work. However, describing how they might *feel* coming to terms with the gap between how it really is and how they thought it would be is quite a challenge.

One mum, Jo, describes the difficulty she had coming to terms with the reality of her baby's sleep and feeding patterns:

> I wish I didn't have such high expectations of when my baby should eat and sleep. I would not have been so frustrated and disappointed when he did what he wanted.

Looking after a baby is hard work, no two ways about it. It's one of the hardest (if not *the* hardest) jobs there is, both physically and emotionally. When a baby isn't feeding and sleeping like the books say they should be, it can seem like an insurmountable mountain for any parent. Knowing those 40-minute not-long-enough naps and 100ml not-big-enough feeds will have no detrimental effect ten years down the track doesn't make it any less stressful at the time.

One parent talked about how she felt coming to terms with her feelings:

> I knew parenting wouldn't be easy, as that's what everyone keeps saying. I thought they meant the lack of sleep, sacrificing a wage, not being able to do things at a minutes' notice, not go out, etc. On that level I felt totally prepared.

> What I didn't know was it's so hard on an emotional level. The guilt. The hormones. The realisation that you want to be the best of the best at your new job but so scared of failing (which happens often, despite how hard you try!) This part was overwhelming, and for a moment I didn't feel worthy of being given such a beautiful gift that was my baby girl.

She also talked about how painful it was coming to terms with not being able to breastfeed:

> "Every mother can breastfeed," my maternal child health nurse said. This was the hardest, as I simply couldn't! Try as I might, there was no milk for my starving baby and my nurse kept telling me off for giving her formula.

> I ended up having to lie to the nurse to get her off my back. "It's working now, she's breastfeeding beautifully,"

which wasn't the case, and it broke my heart to give her formula.

There's so much support for breastfeeding women, but nothing out there but in-your-face guilt if you are unable to breastfeed for any reason.

That was failure number one. A very early one. But I moved on. She's a very healthy, happy child now and it made no difference to her health, as controversial as that sounds.

It's no question: breast milk is always best, and I fully support breastfeeding mothers. But I support bottle-feeding mothers as well.

Becoming a parent is a joyful event. But it can also be a time of struggle, change and confusion. It's a time when we question ourselves and our abilities. Acquiring all these new skills at one time can feel like a massive learning curve (and it *is* massive), yet we all come out the other side with new skills, insights and awareness.

It's okay to struggle at this major junction in our lives. Let yourself struggle without beating yourself up. Out of the challenges will emerge the moments of joy. And it's those moments—where we connect with our kids, partners, friends, family, strangers and *ourselves*—that make life meaningful.

The romanticized version of parenthood we see in the media is *not* an accurate reflection of real life parenting.

When I see expectant parents in the community I show them images of babies and new mums and dads in the nappy commercials. Then I juxtapose those images with a real mum who isn't wearing make-up, isn't pristinely showered and dressed, and looks… well, as if she's just had a baby.

It's really important to acknowledge the difference, and to understand the inferred pressure the media creates. Isolating the source of needing to look and be perfect can be difficult sometimes. But if parents can be a bit easier on themselves, and understand the images we see on TV and in magazines are fantasy, then the pressure is off.

Renee, a lactation consultant, remembers looking at other parents before she became a mum and seeing a peaceful and settled image of motherhood:

> When I was pregnant for the first time, I was blissfully unaware of the journey I was about to embark on. I remember seeing mothers out and about with their babies sleeping peacefully in the pram, or breastfeeding in public, and thinking how hard can it be?
>
> I attended my antenatal hospital education classes, but have no recollection of the issues that can be part of successful breastfeeding, or of normal baby behaviour, or of baby sleep, or about what postnatal support is available if required.

Another mum describes the shock of just how unromantic parenthood was for her:

> Why did it feel so hard? Why did I struggle with my thoughts? Why did I feel like I was failing as a mother? If it wasn't depression or anxiety, what was it?
>
> Looking back, I now know what it was. It's not rocket science or anything, just a combination of exhaustion along with trying to learn many completely new skills, landing in a new social circle with a different body and no clothes that fit. And mixed in with that was losing the comforting routine of my old job, being isolated at home and listening to a screaming baby and smelling that acrid smell of baby vomit.
>
> It felt as if I was somebody else, living someone else's life. It was all so… foreign.
>
> Moving house is rated as one of the most stressful things to do. So it makes sense now that moving or relocating your life to a different planet, the planet of motherhood, is going to hurt a bit.

Nowadays, with families spread out over states (or even countries) and communities more fragmented than ever, our first experience of life with a newborn baby might well be when we're holding our own. And the only other images we see are those in the media, which warp our sense of what is normal.

The truth is that while it's immensely rewarding at times,

parenting can be monotonous, uninspiring, and plain hard work. If you feel this way, you can bet other parents feel this way too. It just means you're normal.

One mum sums up the unromantic reality for her:

> I had not prepared myself for parenthood and being a first time mum at all. I had no idea what it involved. I had this image of a mum holding her quiet baby contently and a "happily ever after" scenario. I didn't expect an unsettled baby, sleepless nights, postnatal depression, and that life as I knew it would be over.

She felt like she'd lost her old self, and wasn't that inspired about life with a new baby.

Sound familiar? It might for some. But it's hard to admit we sometimes feel let down by what is supposed to be such a romantic episode of our lives.

Don't get me wrong—the romance *is* there, in drops and streams. But to ignore that mixed in with it might be trickles of anxiety, puddles of exhaustion and rivers of tears is not presenting a full picture of what normal parenthood can be like.

Pressure may come from outside expectations, but you and your partner are the experts on your baby—nobody else.

As parents, we come to terms with our new reality of having a baby. But while we're juggling our own expectations, we're also hearing (and responding to) the expectations of those around us. And when you're sleep deprived it can be hard to keep doing what's best for your own family unit.

Knowing you're the expert of your own baby lessens the pressure to react to others.

Health professionals (not to mention extended family) can put a lot of expectations on parents. If we're feeling less than confident (which is how many first-time parents feel), we start experiencing the pressure of trying to keep everyone happy.

One mum of two young girls remembers feeling that pressure:

> After our first baby was born, everything in the early weeks felt like a huge blur. It seemed as though I was trying to carry a mountain on my shoulders, as I was faced with such a huge learning curve on top of having so little sleep. I remember having difficulty settling Jessica to sleep, and thinking I was the only mother on the planet with a baby who didn't settle well to sleep.
>
> I started to doubt my innate ability to make enough milk. I remember enduring excruciatingly sore bleeding, cracked nipples. I struggled with anxiety to do with Jessica's weight gains, pressure from extended family members to supplement Jessica with formula, ongoing nipple pain and extreme lack of sleep.
>
> All in all, I felt defeated.

Another mum felt the pressure of her mother-in-law's expectations of how she and her husband should share the load:

> After a while, the little "digs" would start if my husband

sacrificed a night out on the booze in favour of staying home (sometimes with my encouragement). There was no support for what I was doing, going through or sacrificing. Suddenly he was the world's greatest father and husband, and if I wasn't the full Stepford Wife he was apparently suffering. Poor him!

So apparently his life wasn't to change at all because he changed a nappy once. "Wow. No man has ever done that before. Isn't he amazing?" He wasn't to get up through the night "because he has work in the morning", but when I was working it was still up to me. It was very one-sided.

This went on for years and we nearly fell out completely until dear hubby finally saw what was going on and told her to pull her head in!

Family members, friends and even strangers will comment, judge and interfere, and not even a higher power can stop this.

Your only saving grace is you don't need to justify the way you raise your child to anyone. You don't need to react, explain or even give a reason. Just confidently push on the way you see fit. (Not that I'm saying it's easy to do.)

Paul, an investment advisor, distinctly remembers other family members still expecting him to attend family functions and social outings once baby came along:

You hope no-one notices you've lost your rhythm. That your world is moving to a beat you can't control and don't understand. Others don't understand you are dancing to the beat of a different drum. Best you hope for is to cover it up and hope others are either in the same dislocation or don't notice.

It can be a challenge to step up and claim to be The Expert on Your Baby. But you are. You and your partner know what your baby needs and how you need to run as a family. For now, you are your baby's advocate.

Your baby may not be the baby you expected.

We all have expectations and ideas about what sort of parent we want to be. So inevitably we'll have expectations about who our baby will be and how we will relate to them.

I quickly learned that your baby is not half of each parent, putty in your hands to shape. Right from the start, a baby is an individual with their own unique needs, preferences and behaviours.

A midwife who helped me from the maternity ward to the car when my daughter was born said, "Remember your baby is on loan to you". This drove home the message that my baby was a person in her own right—not some imagined image of how I thought a baby *should* look and act like.

Lael, a birth attendant had expectations about how she and her first baby would relate to each other after birth:

> After a labour that dragged on for three days with a birth plan that stated I wanted it to be as natural as possible, I ended up in a system where the cascade of interventions became my default and birth trauma was etched into my being.

When I held Ky for the first time I felt nothing. I was in complete shock and totally overwhelmed around what had just happened to me. I kissed and cuddled my precious baby boy, but I felt nothing. I watched, as my husband cradled our newborn with such love and adoration in his eyes. All I could think was, "I don't feel that".

I was fiercely protective of Ky. I loved him, but I wasn't in love with him. I went through the motions—breastfeeding, caring for him, looking after him—but inside I felt like I was in complete shock.

Each time I sat down to breastfeed him, I'd replay the birth over and over in my mind. I couldn't make sense of what had happened to me, what went wrong and why I felt so shattered. All I knew was that I must be a bad mum. I didn't feel the way you were meant to feel when you had a baby.

The truth is, there's no particular way we *should* feel.

Another mum said that due to severe reflux she didn't start to bond with her baby until he was more than four months old:

My baby would look away from me every time he fed. I had expectations that babies look lovingly into your eyes while they suck away. But my baby was in pain every time he fed, and so he associated me with pain. How could we relate to each other when his own mummy was a source of distress? It was only after he started medication for his reflux that we began to form a connection with each other.

Babies have an inborn temperament, and it might not be the one you expected. You might have an easy going baby, or a highly sensitive one. Your baby may come with a medical condition you didn't expect. Coming to terms and accepting your baby for who they are is essential, but it can be a painful process.

Summary:

The reality of being a parent may be different from what you expected.

Coming to terms with the reality of parenthood may be challenging.

The romanticized version of parenthood we see in the media is not an accurate reflection of real life parenting.

Pressure may come from outside expectations but you and your partner are the experts on your baby—nobody else.

Your baby may not be the baby you expected.

Acknowledging the losses

With any major life transition—moving out of home, marriage, graduating from university, becoming a grandparent for the first time—the experience can be bittersweet.

Moving out of home gives us independence, but we also lose the domestic support of mum doing the washing and cooking for us. A new grandchild may have us mourning our youth. When we marry a loving partner, we may feel we've lost part of our independence.

And having a baby can feel just as bittersweet.

Transition to parenthood involves gains *and* losses.

Becoming a parent is one of the most joyful experiences a person can have. However, as with any transition in life, this new role comes with its fair share of losses. And as a society we often fail to recognise them.

The losses come in many shapes and sizes, including:

- loss of career, income and identity
- loss of social life, time, freedom and friends
- loss of your neat, ordered and simple life when it was just you and your partner.

This difficulty of processing the more painful feelings is widespread. It's easier to ignore the hard parts, turn a blind eye and stick with what feels easier. But when you ignore those nagging feelings you suppress them, and they may emerge as something more sinister such as depression.

Even without feeling depressed, the transition to parenthood can involve some pretty confronting emotions. As one parent expressed to me:

> The funny thing is, I never was diagnosed with postnatal depression. How I would have loved to hear those words— Post. Natal. Depression.—come from the mouths of any of the myriad of health professionals I saw. But apparently I was fine because I didn't meet the criteria for such an illness.
>
> Postnatal depression would have explained everything. But I didn't have that diagnosis to hang my hat on, so I

had to keep looking for a reason why I felt so hopeless.

Now I realise it was okay to be feeling all the losses and resentment I felt, and that did not make me a bad mum.

The point of telling you how I felt is that transitioning to motherhood can be very challenging. Even without the diagnosis of postnatal depression.

It's okay to feel resentment, anger, grief, uncertainty, worry and shock. What isn't helpful is ignoring those feelings.

When we become parents we may experience some losses. But we also gain a tremendous amount of life experience, new friends, and self-awareness.

It also unlocks unseen facets of our personality.

Acknowledging the losses and grieving are essential parts of moving forward.

As well as acknowledging the losses, it's important to let yourself feel the grief. Make space for it, embrace it, and talk about it.

Jo, a mother of two young children, describes how she sought help to allow herself to grieve after a traumatic pregnancy:

At 26 weeks pregnant, working in the Melbourne CBD, I noticed I was leaking fluids.

Something just didn't feel right.

I caught the train to my car, then drove myself to the

hospital for a checkup. Within thirty minutes of arriving at emergency I was told my fluids had broken, I was 3cm dilated, and I'd be giving birth within 12 hours.

This was not how it was supposed to be. Up to this point I'd had a "normal" pregnancy, or at least as normal as the book told me.

I was told my baby had 20% chance of survival and, if it did survive, there was a huge risk of severe medical difficulties and/or disability.

I cried for my unborn baby.

They pumped me full of medication to try and slow down my labour. We waited.

I lay in my hospital bed for nine weeks. I even ate and bathed lying down. I lay there 24 hours a day, only leaving the room (lying down) when they wheeled me off for my next ultrasound.

I kept my baby with me until a day shy of 37 weeks, and he was born a healthy baby boy.

It was a very trying time for my husband. Coming into the hospital daily after work left him with little time for general household chores. When our son was born my muscles had completely vanished due to bed rest. I couldn't walk distances or hold the baby for long periods.

I had to slowly build myself up to cleaning and shopping for groceries.

When he was three months old I knew something wasn't right. My maternal health nurse referred me for counseling. I was diagnosed with Post Traumatic Stress. I had to grieve for my pregnancy, and the emotions I'd kept at bay while I concentrated on growing my baby.

Another mum, Michelle, spoke about the losses she felt as she grieved for what *should* have happened as her baby entered the world:

The birth wasn't natural. But neither was the pregnancy—it was horrible. I went from a 34B bra to a 44DD with a bra extension in the last month. My feet were so swollen I couldn't wear shoes. I went from 52kg to 83kg on the day he was born. I vomited, cried, and felt sick and toxic most of the time.

I was thrilled to be birthing this giant child into the world, and I wanted to do it as naturally as making a huge poo.

But it wasn't like that either.

The birth experience was a nightmare. All I remember is the hospital theatre and a team of green-masked people frantically lifting this breech ten pound boy out into the world.

Breastfeeding didn't happen naturally. The D&C in

my bed post-C-section wasn't part of the plan. And the bleeding nipples and reluctant sucking from big baby didn't factor into my preconceived ideas of what it would be like at all.

Grieving can be a different process for everyone. Some may just need time alone to think and process all the changes. Some may need to talk to a partner or friend. And some may need professional counselling.

Change and loss lead to growth.

The challenges men and women face as they transition from a couple to a family are immense. But without challenges and change, our growth remains stagnant and stunted. It's one of the many transitions we'll face in our lifetime.

Life is a series of transitions—big and small, painful and joyful. We change so we can grow. Without disruption we stay the same—still and unaltered.

Many people who face illness or major life events comment on the gift they've been given in the face of such trauma.

The story below is written by Rachel, who sums up beautifully how her grief led to growth:

The birth of a baby moves you into such a delicate, vulnerable space. The power of such a space is the possibility for illumination of self, of growth and learning.

When I became a mother I was thrown completely out of the reality I'd known and into a new space where I didn't know where or how to be. That's not so unusual, is it? But, in that space of uncertainty, there opened a great potential for learning for me.

My gift was a beautiful baby boy, born with profound cerebral palsy.

The shock of realising the amount of damage in my son's brain left me feeling completely numb. The prognosis they gave us was grim, delivered in the bleakest terms by specialists conditioned by necessity to remain emotionally detached.

I was terrified.

My deep wounds of guilt and self-blame were paralysing. The pain of knowing that somehow, I had carried and borne a beautiful, innocent child who wasn't okay was more than I could bear.

I felt like a failure. I'd failed Oscar as I carried him in my womb and, try as I might, nothing I did now could soothe or settle him.

I felt broken.

My amazing husband moved into the role of "the rock". Unflinchingly positive, he helped any way he could to share the load as our darling Oscar spent most of his young existence crying... screaming.

31

But we fought.

Oscar fought, I fought and my husband fought. How could we not fight for this little man? We watched him work harder than anyone I've ever seen just to survive. The overwhelming feelings of devastation remained, but my Oscar required so much care we both put aside our emotions for a time and moved into survival mode. We held on for dear life. The feelings of panic were never far away—we were in crisis all the time as our beautiful boy fought for life.

He couldn't sleep or feed with any ease. Everything was a struggle, and there was no peace in our home or in our hearts. But somehow we got through those early years, surviving on autopilot with severe lack of sleep and no idea what would come next.

The unfolding of Oscar's story became the unfolding of our story. We moved on, facing the obstacles and challenges that presented themselves to us one by one.

The simple things for Oscar were extremely difficult— basic body functions, learning to eat with a spoon, and simply finding a way to feel comfortable. He needed so much help from us just to manage each day.

As I look back on the progress he's made, I realise it's really about the progress we have made, not just as parents but as people. We've opened our hearts and learned to love fully, without expectation. Loving our beautiful Oscar has exposed us and left us vulnerable—open to hurt, but open to joy as well.

When the demands are great, it's so easy to shut down, develop a hardness to cope, to protect ourselves from the pain. And it is painful watching Oscar struggle with his body day after day, night after night.

But as the years have progressed I've learned to open myself more deeply to the experience. To allow him to show me his wisdom. He's shown me how to trust the experience I'm having. How to trust the experience he's having, even though it's often so difficult to watch.

We have so many scary moments with Oscar. Parenting him never feels safe or secure. But when we emerge from a more intense time with him, the learnings are tangible. We laugh gently at ourselves as we are shown another way we've been resisting, trying to control the uncontrollable… life!

Oscar is 12. He will never speak, will never walk, and will need us to care for him for the rest of his life. He's fragile, and his little body won't sustain him for much longer. We will lose him, sometime.

But his many gifts will remain, and he has given us so much. He has shown me how strong I am. He has taught me patience. He has given me the gift of perspective. I am truly blessed to be able to witness his strength, his grace.

I feel like one of the lucky ones.

I feel honoured to be his mother. I wouldn't change anything about him, and I wouldn't change anything about my experience as a mum. It's not always easy or enjoyable, and I'm certainly not always at my best within it. But I am richer for it.

Summary:

Transition to parenthood involves gains and losses.

Acknowledging the losses and grieving are essential parts of moving forward.

Change and loss lead to growth.

Changing roles

Being a parent is a new position you may never have considered filling before. As with any role, whether it's in the workplace or in your community, there are mandatory criteria, essential skills, and other skills that would make the job easier.

Your new role as parent may feel as foreign as your first day at a new office. You may even feel like a junior member of the team for quite some time.

But with time you will become a parent. And you'll be able to claim back (or totally re-invent) the aspects of yourself that may have been lost in the process.

Becoming a different version of "me" may take some time.

It's common to feel confused, even stunned, about where you fit in once baby comes along. Creating a family after you've established a career can make the role change even more challenging.

Even changing roles from pregnant lady to postnatal mum can make a mother feel invisible. When all the attention suddenly switches from the blossoming mum to the new baby, it can feel like she no longer matters.

As Michelle, a mum and personal trainer, recounts:

> When Millie was about nine months old, I felt I really had a handle on the mothering gig. She was sleeping through the night, eating solids, and we both enjoyed breastfeeding and our time together. Instead of mothering taking every waking moment I could not only come up for air, but also look around at my new world where I was now a mother.

> Around this time I started taking Millie to a baby and toddler music group, run by a young energetic woman who got us interacting with our babies and each other with music and movement.

> But something disturbing happened at these sessions: I was always referred to as "Millie's mummy." She never learnt my name, or attempted to use it.

> For the first few sessions I thought it was quite cute. But as we walked home each week, the name "Millie's mummy"

sat like a weight around my shoulders.

Was this who I was now—"Millie's mummy"? What about Mish? What about my education? My work achievements? My identity?

Millie was just at the start of her life. What if I had more children? Would I be buried further in mummy-hood, never to be seen again?

Michelle resolved this identity crisis by looking outwards and seeing how other mums came full-circle and created new versions of themselves.

Which is exactly what she did herself:

So what changed? Life went on. I had another child and immersed myself further into full-time motherhood.

But I looked for role models. Women who went on to have a second career after having children, or who achieved something significant. And it held more weight, because while their life was never truly their own they went and did it anyway.

I read bios of these women. I made friends with them. And in time I became one of them.

Lael talks about losing her identity and feeling almost invisible:

I felt like the constant servitude of motherhood was

smothering me. I wasn't prepared for the feeling of giving up who I thought I was. My ego was starting to die. The person I was before having a baby no longer existed.

I fought against it for a while, holding onto my work image to give me a sense of purpose. Everywhere I looked, the mother archetype was one of invisibility. No-one paid much attention to them, no-one regarded their job as the most important, and no-one whistled as I walked down the street pushing a pram!

I felt lost. I didn't know who I was as a woman anymore. And through all this searching, Ky bore the brunt of my confusion.

I was angry no-one told me about this loss of identity. I was furious mothers weren't held in higher regard as the ones shaping the next generation. I felt betrayed by society.

And even though I looked okay on the outside, I was completely lost.

Lael looked inwards, and learned to grow into and accept her new role. But it took some time:

I softened as a mother and began to feel comfortable in my own shoes. I started observing how my relationship with my children was ever-evolving and constantly changing.

Even though we give birth to a baby in a matter of hours, it can take much longer, sometimes years, to develop into the role of a parent.

Becoming a parent puts us on a huge learning curve. You learn a lot of new skills, take in a lot of information, and expend a lot of emotional energy. And it certainly doesn't happen overnight.

So go easy on yourself. Remember: you've never done this before.

My partner is a dad! Dads matter too.

In the traditional family, the father maintains a similar schedule to the one he had before. But he still experiences a massive shift in where his role lies in the family.

Danny's whole identity as a concert pianist literally disappeared overnight as he felt pressured to be the provider more than anything else:

> Archi came along when I was 23 and still studying at uni. I went from travelling around as a concert pianist without much responsibility to being a father with an enormous responsibility.

> It was certainly emotionally challenging. I was forced to put my career aside (due to my not-so-great financial situation) to find a more financially reliable job. I'd studied for 21 years to become a concert pianist—my passion— and had to let it go pretty much overnight.

> My grandmother, aware of my capacity as a musician, bought me some recording equipment. She thought I

could financially provide for Archi by starting a freelance recording studio at home.

My transition to fatherhood effectively redefined my entire direction in life, lifestyle, and career.

The importance of the dad's emotional wellbeing is being recognised more and more. Dads are also vulnerable during this time, and if the mum becomes depressed there's a high risk of the dad being diagnosed with depression as well.

Men often hold the fort while their partner acclimatises to life with a new baby, so they can't seek the support they need. They don't often have the same contact women have with other parents and health professionals, and so are left with little support during this time.

Barry, a trained engineer and new father, suddenly realised he had no training behind him to be a dad:

The midwife and staff were reassuring me everything was okay and how it should be. I'm a structural engineer. What do I know about having babies?

I spent the next few days between hospital and celebrating with friends and family. It was all a bit of a blur, but such an exciting time of my life.

After three days I realised I hadn't been home yet, and should feed the dog. Wow, what sort of a parent will I be?

Barry was struck by the sheer sense of responsibility he now had.

Extended family also take on new roles.

Mum and dad aren't the only ones taking on a new role. Parents become grandparents, sisters become aunties and brothers become uncles. The shift in roles sends a ripple (or sometimes a tsunami) right through the extended family. And we often forget that other family members may also find their new role challenging.

We often have expectations of each other in our new roles. As one parent commented:

> I thought my mum would be a doting grandmother, wanting to be with my kids at the drop of a hat. But she showed less interest than I could ever have imagined. It was a painful process to realise that how she took on her role as grandmother was beyond my control.

It works the other way too. Grandparents often have expectations of how much involvement they'll have with their grandchildren, and sometimes there's a mismatch between what the parents want and what the grandparents want.

One mother of three was overwhelmed how the birth of her baby girl caused a role shift in every generation of the family:

> I knew I was having a girl the second time around, and I never thought about how much impact another generation of women would have. But when I was in labour, I became incredibly overwhelmed thinking about the lineage of women in my family.

My mother was at the birth, and I called for her to stand beside me. In tears I blubbered, "I am your daughter and I'm having a daughter and I am her mother and you are my mother". Tears streamed down our faces as we shared this moment.

I'm not sure anyone else in the room quite got the impact of this. But it was the beginning of a monumental change in who I wanted to be.

Summary:

Becoming a different version of "me" may take some time.

My partner is a dad! Dads matter too.

Extended family also take on new roles.

CHAPTER
4

Relationship changes

In any scenario where two becomes three, the dynamics are going to change. After all, three's a crowd.

As adults (and parents) we need to figure out a way to make it work. With time, patience and some skills to handle the conflict (yes, it's okay to have conflict), the relationship can come through unscathed.

A good way to start managing any conflicts that surface is to understand you both come from different families where values may differ.

Your relationship with your partner will change.

It's common for new dads to feel resentful and left out when a new baby arrives. Up until this point it's just been the two of you, and now you are a family. Becoming a family is a massive transition, and shouldn't be underestimated.

One mum became aware of how important it was to listen to her partner with empathy:

> My relationship with my husband became… well, different. I think the main difference was our marriage took on a new meaning and purpose. Every thought and action now revolves around our children's needs. Our children are our reason for being. This can be very empowering, but also very daunting.

> Talking about my feelings in a non-judgemental way with my husband, and being empathetic to his feelings/needs, have been very important in keeping our relationship strong. You're in this journey together. Sometimes men and women feel like they're worlds apart, but deep down they usually have the same values. It's a matter of communicating, using empathy and active listening, to find that common ground.

Couples experience losses and gains just as individuals do. Parts of their relationship may seem lost, yet other aspects of their relationship may flourish.

This could be a challenging time of transition for you both.

This quote, from a parent of an extremely unsettled baby, accurately reflects how exhaustion and transition can have an impact on your relationship:

> By week four, our household was not stable at all. It affected every relationship in the house.

Another mum comments on how her relationship took a back seat to the baby and her toddler:

> After the birth of our second son I said to my husband, "It's a good thing we like each other," because we hadn't had a proper conversation, hugged or even acknowledged each other in weeks.

> Having a new baby is bloody hard on a relationship, but like all things is a phase that passes.

It's incredibly common for partners to feel disconnected around this time. In fact, one well regarded study* states that one in two couples rate the quality of their marriage at this time as "in decline".

Remember: it's not just you.

It's okay to have a bit of space between you and your partner (you pretty much *have* to make some space for this new person to be in). But making an effort to reconnect when the baby isn't so dependent on mum any more is important.

And newborn babies really *are* dependant. Human beings are the most vulnerable of all mammals—think how other mammals can stand and walk as soon as they're born.

Try to remember it won't be like this forever. Your baby will grow bigger and stronger, and soon you'll be able to leave him or her with other people while you reconnect with each other.

It's common to feel less intimacy between you and your partner when bub is on the scene. Mum often has so much physical contact with the baby during the day that any more seems just too much. It's hard not to take this personally. She just needs a little bit of space.

As one mum comments:

> My husband demanded sex six weeks to the day after giving birth to our first son. I could easily have waited another six years.

And that just about sums up how a lot of women feel.

Your partner may do things differently—don't shut them out.

I often talk about mum becoming "the gatekeeper", when mum feels she knows better than her partner at all costs.

When dad tries to help with caring for the baby he can't live up to mum's standards and is criticised for the way he does things. Eventually he's pushed away, and he gives up offering to help. And mum feels as if she has no help or support.

The alternative is learning to accept that your partner may look after baby in a different way. Challenge yourself to believe it won't harm or affect the baby in any way, and let go of the reigns of control.

I'm not saying it's easy to do. For some it can be a difficult and painful process.

One mum sums it up so well:

> Accept that your partner may want to do things differently. Let him, and only come to the rescue if he asks or if it's really necessary. There's no "right" or "wrong" when it comes to parenting. You're both on a steep learning curve.

Wise but challenging advice for many.

Ask yourself, "What's the worst that can happen if they put the baby down five minutes later than I would have?" Be curious and ask, "Does it *really* matter if they wrap the baby in a different way?" Be bold and see what happens when the answer is, "No, it really doesn't".

Letting go of the reigns can be a challenge. But it's one you may be willing to face

Summary:

Your relationship with your partner will change.

This could be a challenging time of transition for you both.

Your partner may do things differently—don't shut them out.

*Belsky J, Kelly J. Why some couples grow closer and others apart. New York: Dell; 1994. The transition to parenthood: How a first child changes a marriage.

CHAPTER

5

Family of origin

Many people who've had a regular upbringing see their families as "The Gold Standard". Even children who've had an unusual or abusive upbringing see it as "normal" because it's the only version of family they've ever known.

But once you become a parent yourself, you may realise your parents weren't so perfect after all. And that can often be a difficult thing to accept.

(By the way, your children will discover your flaws sooner or later, so you may as well just fess up now and tell them that nobody's perfect.)

Your childhood matters.

Your family of origin (the family you grew up with) will have a major impact on how you feel and function as a new parent.

Many new parents are shocked at how significant and powerful their childhood memories can be around this time. We may start questioning how we were parented, and what impact it had on us—and could have on our own children.

One brave and insightful mum who took on the painful task of looking back to her childhood said:

> I'm a very happy woman. I have the man of my dreams, two beautiful children, a house with a pool near the beach, wonderful friends and a successful business that disrupts our family life very little.
>
> My childhood was very turbulent and lonely. But I left it all behind, determined not to carry that baggage with me. I wanted to enjoy the present, look forward to the future, and not repeat the mistakes of my parents.
>
> And I wanted to forgive them for the mistakes they made, because they must have also had these emotions, right? We're all doing the best we can, and we're all going to make mistakes.
>
> So many emotions came flooding back.
>
> Part of it was anger at my own parents for allowing me to go through so much, and go through it alone. I was an only child from an unplanned teenage pregnancy, so my

parents (who weren't together) were young and selfish. My mother was beautiful and very attractive (even now people comment on how stunning she is), and I could see the disappointment in people's faces when they looked at me.

I wasn't beautiful.

I wasn't popular either. I could never maintain a friendship, partly because we moved every year. (I went to 12 different primary schools.) I was once abused while in the "care" of somebody else. Later I discovered he was known for this behaviour, but I was still left with him which hurt me deeply. I was emotionally neglected, and had no-one to turn to.

My teenage years were filled with depression. But I knew the life I wanted and was determined to make it happen, so I got on with it. I worked hard, finished high school, and started earning money working at McDonald's. Eventually I made some brilliant friends at school. They're still my friends, and understand and support me completely.

My mother was always out partying, so I did it all on my own. As hard as it was, there were some positives. I'm very independent, can stand on my own two feet, and can support myself financially.

I grew up quickly.

I'd forgotten about all those negative feelings—I buried

them all so deep—until quite recently. You know the saying, "You never appreciate your parents until you become one yourself"? Well, my experience was the opposite. I constantly stuck up for my parents, loved them with all my heart, and was constantly reminded how well they did considering they had me so young. And for the most part, they did.

But once I became a parent, I saw the cracks. I realised how terrible they were at taking care of me, because they really didn't take care of me at all. I existed, and that was about it. My family, my darling grandmother and some aunties gave me lots of love, and I credit them a lot for how I turned out.

Dealing with the emotions of the past, and realising how crap my parents truly were, was a very tough pill to swallow. Don't get me wrong—there were many good times in there as well. Unfortunately the bad times outweigh them.

Some choose not to look back at their childhood, and so never understand those niggling feelings of discomfort, those patterns of behaviour or irrational thoughts. For others, the issues may not be as painful as this mum's story.

What matters most is becoming aware of how the family you grew up with functioned and related to each other, especially in times of stress. Which parts of your childhood family will you bring to your new family, and which parts will you leave out? Have you asked your partner the same question about their childhood family?

Unpacking the details of your childhood may be challenging and painful.

While it's all well and good to say it helps to know where you've come from, coming to this point in awareness can be very unsettling.

Lisa, a chiropractor and mum of two young girls, explains how challenging it was for her:

> A lot of the painful feelings I had to deal with related to my family of origin—the family I grew up in.
>
> Funnily enough, I thought I'd managed to squish any thoughts or painful feelings about my family into a tiny little forgotten ball in the pit of my stomach. But life has a way of allowing those painful feelings to seep out at the edges.
>
> Having a baby was the catalyst that forced me to deal with those feelings.
>
> I seemed to have obsessive thoughts about my upbringing every day, if not every hour. I'd pace the streets and pound the pavement with my unsettled baby, my mind moving faster than my feet.
>
> I looked at women walking with their newborn on a sunny day and would think how relaxing and pleasant it seemed. Then I reminded myself how uncomfortable those walks were. I felt hot, agitated, sped up, uncentred, off-balance,

troubled, *angry*. They were far from pleasant.

So what was I pondering on those walks? What was making me feel so angry? Here's an excerpt from my journal (where I refer to my baby) that may help explain it:

> *My mum called me "difficult" for as long as I can remember, and her labelling did a lot of damage.*
>
> *I'm acutely aware you have a similar temperament to mine. You're not difficult. You're vivacious, fiery, entertaining, delightful and charming.*

My mother found me difficult to parent for her own reasons, but put the label on me.

I don't hold any of this against her now. She was doing her best.

It took a long time to let go of my anger towards her. At times I felt I was healing, but then she'd do something (like trying to label my daughter as "difficult, just like you were") and my anger would escalate.

But once I understood her painful past it was easier to understand her—her black-and-white thinking, her critical nature, her inability to show emotion.

This is how the family you came from can create myths about its members. The myth in my family was I was a difficult person, but the truth (and a huge "A-ha!" moment for me as an adult) is that I wasn't a difficult person at all. My mother just found me difficult to parent—a completely different thing.

My mum was driven to be a good mother (whatever that is), but because of my fiery nature I didn't fit into her perfect picture of motherhood. I couldn't heal the hurts of her past, and I couldn't let her be the perfect mother because of my temperament, and so in her eyes I was difficult.

To be a parent to my own child and not pass down the same labelling system I had to deal with, I needed to turn inward and discard this myth, and the label of "difficult person." A lot of the anger came from having to deal with all this "stuff" because my mum couldn't deal with *her* issues and passed them down to me.

I'm happy to say I no longer obsess over my mum and what I wish I'd had. I'm more accepting of who she is, where she came from, and why she needed to label me. But it's a fine balance, and I'm trying not to overcompensate with demonstrating love and closeness when it comes to my own children.

The pain still resurfaces from time to time, but it's manageable. And because I'm aware of the issues in the family I grew up in, I'm providing a better template for my kids.

Parents who choose to confront issues from their own childhood head-on will come through at the other end feeling lighter, more self aware, and much less agitated and anxious.

Differentiating from your family of origin can be empowering.

One mum looked deeply at what she learnt from her own mother and made a conscious decision about what to take with her and what to discard:

> I'd always thought of myself as a masculine woman. Being deeply influenced by my own mother, I began to analyse what I'd learned from her.
>
> There was so much I was grateful for. My strength, courage and faith in the world. A belief that I can do anything I want. A passion to follow my dreams, and a big heart that will always help anyone in need.
>
> But I also noticed this very strong lineage of women had forgotten the subtle gifts of the feminine along the way. The ability to be truly vulnerable, and to honour yourself with a break when you need it. The softness that comes from being with women in a slow, intimate setting sharing their stories, dreams and visions. The deep acceptance of the woman's body in all its forms.
>
> As I looked down at my sleeping daughter, I realised a great deal had to change. And it had to start with me. I

made a conscious decision to start balancing the feminine in me. What I wanted for her, I first had to change, heal and honour within myself.

Being self-aware is a one of the best gifts you can give to your child.

Summary:

Your childhood matters.

Unpacking the details of your childhood may be challenging and painful.

Differentiating from your family of origin can be empowering.

CHAPTER 6

Priorities

Before baby arrived, we had plenty of time to do everything. We valued our freedom and spontaneity, but didn't really notice it because we... well, took it for granted.

Babies are hard work, and can take up a lot of our time. While we do it out of love, it's okay to resent struggling to find some time for ourselves.

Finding that time is a priority.

Juggling the load can be a challenge. We can't do it all, and that's okay.

Some women find it hard to manage the demands placed on them. A common concern is feeling they're letting somebody down. "If I say I'll do something, then I must do it." The perfectionist in many us drives us to be Supermum or Superdad.

One parent talked about the frustration of feeling pulled between her kids and her work:

Last week I had to face my worst fears.

I woke up, excited about presenting my workshop to a few mums and professionals. It had taken me a full month (and a lot of effort) to plan.

As I got dressed, I heard a cough coming from the room of my three-year-old and tried to ignore it. Ten minutes later both kids were up and complaining they weren't feeling well. Neither of them wanted breakfast, which is usually a good indicator they aren't well.

I started to panic.

I called my husband, but he couldn't help out. Last-minute babysitters and neighbours weren't an option either.

I hadn't planned for the possibility of my kids being sick.

After a few tears, I realised there was no other option but

to cancel the workshop. My kids will always come first, but my work is valuable too. And the pain of having to let a group of people down made it a really tough day.

But I learned that on the whole people are forgiving and understanding. And although I find it had to let people down, it's not the end of the world.

Allowing ourselves to be human takes the pressure off.

Two very powerful words we can say to ourselves are, "Oh, well". I often mutter those words. "Oh, well. I didn't get the chores done today", "Oh, well. I'll need to cancel that appointment today", etc. I'm not saying it's easy. It can be a challenge to let go of control and embrace the chaos of living with a young baby or child.

You matter.

If there's one thing you must (and can) control when you have a baby, it's putting time aside for yourself. If you don't stop and refuel, you'll burn out. What other job needs you available 24 hours a day?

One mum helped herself by putting firmer boundaries in place:

I started saying "No" more to people when my soul told me I needed quiet more that I needed to save the world.

Another mum, Anna, says the mess has to be a lower priority so she can be a higher priority:

Accept that mess will happen. Don't worry—your little one will not only survive, but also contribute significantly to its creation later on.

One of the biggest hurdles stopping mums taking time out for themselves is guilt. Michelle, a mum, says:

I'd look at other mothers and wonder if they mourned the loss of their identity too. Or did they just get used to their new identity?

I wanted to know if I got myself back.

It was hard to articulate this without either sounding post-natally depressed (which I didn't think I was) or feeling guilty for wanting to put myself over my child.

The truth is, we're better parents if we can take a little regular time for ourselves. We come back refreshed, re-energised, and with a little bit of pleasure under our belts. Without that break, resentment sets in. And that doesn't help anyone.

If mum and dad are okay then baby will be okay.

In the chapter on relationships we talked about the importance of making time for you and your partner. Many an expert has commented that if the parents are okay then the children will be okay too.

But being okay doesn't mean there won't be conflict. It means you may need to step up and face any conflict head on. After all, you and your partner come from two different families with different values. How can there not be conflict around how to parent your children?

Elly, a mum and author, describes how she came to terms with changing after becoming a mum, and how this new version of her affected her relationship with her husband:

> When I first became a mother I felt like Alice going down the rabbit hole—freefalling. I found myself in a weird and wonderful world where I didn't know my way around or have any sense of direction.

> I thought I was really well prepared for motherhood. I'd done the classes and read the books. But nothing prepared me for the two biggest challenges I found becoming a mum.

> Yes, I expected to fall in love with my baby. But I didn't expect the feeling to be so all-encompassing that my feelings toward my husband would pale in comparison. It felt like I was letting him go.

> I still feel sad when I think about that, but I saw no other choice. I was a mother now.

> I didn't expect to feel I was losing myself, either. I was so focused on the baby, and getting him into a routine to get a sense of control, that I didn't make time to do the things that made me... well, *me*.

For a while it felt like I didn't know who I was anymore. I was confused and irritated with myself. And because I couldn't put what was happening into words, it created friction between my husband and me.

Then we lost two babies, which brought us close together again. It felt like our love changed depending on our circumstances. I started to wonder if there was a bigger picture we weren't even aware of. Becoming a mother had the potential to change not only me, but also my relationship with my husband. Since I'd learned that change was also an opportunity for growth, it both frightened and excited me.

I'd always been interested in personal growth. I struggled with depression in my teens, and had done some courses and lots of reading. Now it was dawning on me that becoming a mother was a real catalyst. I was on was an emotional journey, and when I talked to my friends I found they were on a similar (and just as confusing) path.

So it seemed I had two choices. I could struggle with it, fight against it (as I had been), and try and get things back to some sort of "normal". Or it could be an opportunity to learn more about my newly-emerging mother-self and its limits. I could then expand these limits when I could, just learn to say "no" or ask for help when I couldn't.

I worried how this would affect my relationship with my husband, knowing that when we change we change our relationship.

When I was pregnant with our second baby I worked as a relationship counsellor, and many of my clients were going through the same thing. That's when I had my "light bulb" moment: If we were all struggling in the same ways then at least we were "normal".

And then I wondered: With all the preparation I'd done for parenthood, why didn't any of it prepare me for this?

Normalizing the conflict between partners is essential. It's not something that only happens to you. It's common, and makes sense. It's just not often talked about.

Sometimes this struggle passes with time and good communication. Sometimes outside help may be needed.

Being a good enough parent is good enough.

It's common to put on a façade and pretend everything is perfect. We generally don't talk about the challenges of taking care of a young baby, so parents often feel isolated in what they're feeling, as if they're the only ones.

One dad, Barry, says:

People would drop in for a visit. It didn't bother me that the house was messy or chores were piling up. Some of them had babies themselves. They seemed to be coping fantastically, which just made us feel even more inadequate.

He then goes on to describe an almost mask-like quality his wife put on for visitors:

Carol made a big effort to sound really upbeat and in control while the visitors were there, and then would be totally exhausted and drained once they left. We talked about these issues, but she just couldn't get motivated to do anything. Everything was such an ordeal, and it all seemed too much to cope with.

We had too much pride to ask anyone for help, and were too embarrassed to admit we just weren't coping.

If I had a dollar for every time a woman asked me, "Everyone else in my mother's group is managing, so why aren't I?", I'd be a wealthy woman.

Maybe she just happened to catch another parent on a good day. Or maybe it's because no-one is game enough to say, "This is uninspiring, hard work and I want a break."

After all, no-one wants to be judged.

Summary:

Juggling the load can be a challenge. We can't do it all and that's okay.

You matter.

If mum and dad are okay then baby will be okay.

Being a good enough parent is good enough.

CHAPTER

7

Mental health awareness

Awareness is empowerment. The perinatal period can be a fragile time for both women and men. Being prepared is half the battle. The other half is asking for help.

Having a baby is about more than just the birth.

Most couples focus on the labour and the birth of their baby and tend not to think beyond this event. But while it's understandable, we should also consider thinking about what comes next.

The way new parents might *feel* is often ignored. Many sit at home, isolated in their own thoughts and feelings, convinced they're the only ones who think it's a bittersweet experience.

And their feelings can be *so* mixed. "Yes, I love the baby. But this isn't how I thought it would be."

Imagine if we could normalise those early thoughts and feelings? If someone said to every new parent, "You know what? It's okay to feel uninspired, or to see this job as mundane at times". Most of the talk is about the joy (which of course *is* there), but ignoring the reality is doing ourselves a disservice.

One mum explains how she, like most of us, didn't think beyond the birth:

> My husband and I had been trying to have a baby for a number of years, without success. We'd just about given up when I finally fell pregnant.

> Throughout my pregnancy my only concern was to have a healthy baby. I took each day as it came, not wanting to think too far ahead in case anything went wrong.

> When the day finally came to have the baby, I had an elective caesarean. I still did not allow myself to think past the birth. I remember lying in the operating room and

hearing the obstetrician say, "It's a boy". I held my breath, waiting to get the all-clear from the paediatrician.

When I heard him say he's a healthy boy, I just blew a sigh of relief, thinking *It's over. Now I can have a rest.*

Boy, was I wrong!

Marianne remembers dismissing the information about depression, the birth being a higher priority for her:

I was overwhelmed by emotion watching the birth video with my husband at our pre-natal class. But I dismissed the small segment on depression because it had little relevance to me or my husband. As a lawyer, my mind had always been strong, and I'd always been a reasonably high achiever. Depression simply wasn't on my agenda.

This is a common response to hearing about depression. But one in seven women will be diagnosed with postnatal depression (PND), and even more with postnatal anxiety. One in twenty men will be diagnosed with the illness, the biggest risk factor for them being having a partner with the illness.

Another mum with a long history of depression and anxiety thought motherhood might make her immune to a relapse:

I had a history of depression and anxiety before becoming a mother, but I managed very well with medication during my three pregnancies and post birth. In fact, I felt invincible. I felt that, now I was a mother, nothing could get between me and looking after my kids.

How wrong I was.

A history of mental illness is one of the biggest risk factors for PND, no matter how long ago it was. If you're in this situation, it can help to find support as soon as you conceive.

Postnatal depression is a hard diagnosis to make.

If you're concerned about postnatal depression or anxiety, it's a good idea to speak to a GP or a psychologist, even if just for reassurance. It's often a challenge even for health professionals to make the diagnosis, so it's not worth wondering and suffering alone.

When it comes down to it, the label or the diagnosis doesn't matter anyway. Whether it's called postnatal depression or "postnatal this sucks", what matters is you don't feel quite right and with help you can feel better.

One new dad, an engineer, describes how his wife was out of sorts:

> Carol wasn't sleeping well in hospital. She seemed quite anxious about irrelevant things, and still looked washed out four or five days after the birth. She couldn't eat, and was worried about breastfeeding, whether the baby was getting enough milk, etc. I'd never seen her like this, but assumed it was because of the traumatic birth. The doctor put it all down to exhaustion.

The day we left hospital, Carol said she didn't want to come home. The nurses and I thought it must have been the baby blues, and that she'd snap out of it when she got home and could get some sleep and rest.

No one realised she was still in shock after the birth.

No wonder the feelings we have after becoming parents are so confusing. In this scenario three different people thought this man's wife was out of sorts for different reasons. Was it trauma, exhaustion or the baby blues?

If you have any concerns, talk to a professional with experience in this area. (Later on you'll find some resources you can contact for help.)

Awareness is half the battle. Empower yourself with knowledge.

Knowing the risk factors and symptoms of depression and anxiety means you can seek help early.

One mum didn't recognise she had many of the risk factors until much later:

> Three and a half years later, and with the benefit of hindsight, I now realise I had many of the risk factors.
>
> Anxiety and depression had been skirting around the edges of my life for a very long time. The stress of birth, exhaustion, hormone changes, sleep deprivation and the responsibility of caring for a newborn were simply

catalysts. This episode of major depressive illness could have happened at any highly-stressful time in my life.

Genetic vulnerability lit the match, and stressful life events started the fire.

These two information boxes detail the causes and symptoms of postnatal depression. Of course, depression and anxiety manifest differently for different people. And women often don't think they're depressed—they just feel "irritable". Irritability is a common symptom of postnatal depression.

CAUSES/RISK FACTORS FOR POSTNATAL DEPRESSION

BIOLOGICAL

Genetic predisposition

Hormones

Pregnancy complications (mum or baby)

Difficult labour

PSYCHOLOGICAL

History of depression (even if the depression was a long time ago)

Relationship problems

History of abuse

Low self esteem

Recent grief

Unrealistic expectations

Perfectionist traits

SOCIAL

Poor relationship with partner (or no partner)

Lack of support

Financial issues

Moving house

Isolation

Note: This is only an overview, and may not be a complete list.

SYMPTOMS OF DEPRESSION

For a diagnosis of depression, a person usually has four or more symptoms present for most of the time over more than two weeks. The symptoms interrupt the way that person normally functions.

PHYSICAL

Sleep problems

Appetite changes

Panic attacks

No energy

Decreased libido

Physical ailments (e.g. headaches)

Extreme fatigue/hyperactive

PSYCHOLOGICAL

Anxiety/agitation/irritability/anxiety re baby

Persistent sadness

No pleasure or joy

Thoughts of death/suicide/harm to baby

Obsessive thoughts

Guilt/blame/anger

Lack of motivation

Cognitive difficulties—unable to make decisions

Teary

Overwhelmed

Loss of confidence

SYMPTOMS OF DEPRESSION continued
SOCIAL
Avoidance and withdrawal
Fear of being alone
Fear of going out
Dependant on others
Strained relationships
Loss of wider social networks

Note: This is only an overview, and may not be a complete list.

Anxiety and irritability are common too.

There's a lot of media coverage about postnatal depression, but very little about anxiety. But anxiety is far more common than depression, and can exist on its own or in combination with depression.

A common symptom of postnatal depression is irritability. Women often feel they're okay because they don't feel sad, but they still feel irritable and anxious. Anxiety is hard to live with, but with help the symptoms can be treated.

One parent describes just how hard it was to live with her anxiety and irritability:

> I'm usually fairly calm and in control of my emotions. (I once won an award at work for "never spitting the dummy".)

But I got extremely angry when I thought my husband was ignoring my concerns about visiting his parents when our daughter was five weeks old. I felt pressured, and remember screaming at him "You're not listening!" before jumping out of the car at traffic lights and running down the street crying. I felt I had no control over myself, and kept thinking *I haven't felt this way since I was a teenager.*

I still have bouts of anger episodes where I think, say and do things I normally wouldn't dream of doing. And of course later I look back and think *What was I thinking?*

I now understand that irritability and anger can be symptoms of a mood disorder.

She also talks about how she felt when she became anxious:

The physical symptoms of anxiety became so intense my heart was racing 24 hours a day.

I had other symptoms too: racing thoughts, insomnia, sweating, flushes, shaking, shivering, and sore muscles. It felt like adrenalin was coursing through my body all the time, my body "buzzed" as if filled with electricity, and I felt extremely on edge.

Coming through the other side can seem like a gift.

Many women come through the dark tunnel of depression and/

or anxiety and come out the other end with a grateful glow about them. They say the illness gave them an opportunity to look deeper, ask questions, explore their beliefs and bring about change. One mum says:

> The pain of depression was the most profound and enduring form of suffering I've ever experienced. It's certainly been the most challenging thing I've ever confronted, and tested my patience and perseverance beyond measure.

> Having said that, the experience wasn't all bad. I learned things about myself and others, made new friends along the way, and experienced great joy through the love and support of my husband, daughter, family and friends. And support sometimes came from unexpected quarters.

> I gained insight and empathy into a health issue that had a significant impact on my life, and the lives of many others. I'm now more understanding and compassionate, and passionately promote its awareness.

> I learned the causes of depression can be complex and multi-tiered, and that wisdom, time and discernment are usually needed for proper diagnosis and treatment.

> I also learned that depression is a spectrum illness. The symptoms and duration can vary from mild to severe. And despite the term "mental illness", depression can be biological or physical in nature, changing the chemical makeup of the brain to produce very physical symptoms.

Few parents would think deciding to create a family would open up painful wounds. Few would think having a baby would put them in a vulnerable risk group for mental illness. And few could predict how that illness is associated with becoming a parent.

But for many, those statements are the reality. And for most, there is recovery and light at the end of the tunnel.

Summary:

Having a baby is about more than just the birth.

Postnatal depression is a hard diagnosis to make.

Awareness is half the battle. Empower yourself with knowledge.

Anxiety and irritability are common too.

Coming through the other side can seem like a gift.

8

Getting rid of irrational thoughts and being a good enough mum!

A common misunderstanding among people is that it's the events in our lives that make us sad.

We can't change the past. But chances are the events didn't make you feel like rubbish anyway. It's the irrational thoughts you had about the events that generated the negative feelings. And the good news is you can learn to change the way you think.

There's no such thing as "should".

Irrational thoughts are the voices we hear in our head convincing us that something (usually something negative) is true. As human beings we engage in many types of irrational thinking. Entire books have been devoted to this topic. But one aspect of irrational thinking common to new parents is "should" thinking.

When we impose the word "should" on ourselves, it creates a rigid set of expectations. It puts unreasonable demands on ourselves and the rest of the world.

New and pregnant mums are especially good at being hard on themselves—"I should be able to breastfeed", "I should be able to settle my baby", etc.

Why should you? You've never done these things before, they're completely new skills. We wouldn't be so hard on ourselves if we were learning a skill unrelated to parenthood. How many people learning to roller-skate fall down and demand they "should" be able to skate?

Are you a "should" thinker? Being aware of irrational thinking (such as "should" thinking), and challenging your self-talk and the way you think, is a way to start being softer on yourself.

One mum describes how she tried eradicating the word "should" from her vocabulary:

> It's just a six-letter word. But for me it was a pretty dangerous word, and led to a lot of irrational thinking.
>
> It took me a long time to realise that when it comes to mothering (or anything else in life), there's no such thing as "should".

It's a word that creates rigid expectations on yourself and others. And using it was setting myself up for failure.

Not only was I using it myself, I was also using it with everyone around me.

My mum should help out more with the baby.

My mother-in-law should give me more space.

My dog should stop asking me for attention.

My husband should be able to read my mind.

I slowly isolated myself because it felt like everyone was letting me down.

Trying to control everyone with "should" was exhausting, and I soon realised the only thing I *could* control was my reaction to what was happening around me.

Sometimes it was painful to see that reality wasn't as I wanted it to be. But it was real, and nowhere near as exhausting as trying to control everything and everyone around me.

For this mum, the lesser evil was to relinquish control and accept there really are no "shoulds".

Negative thinking can be managed with tools: mindfulness and cognitive behaviour therapy (CBT).

In chapter 11 I'll be talking about mindful parenting, and how it relates to connecting with your baby. But it can also be used to combat negative thinking.

In a nutshell, being mindful means:

- focussing on the present, rather than the future (what if) or the past (what was)
- understanding you are not your thoughts, and letting go of negative thoughts instead of buying into them
- being flexible in our parenting
- being emotionally present for our babies when they need us
- being less reactive.

Seana, an author and mum of four, uses the mindfulness technique to help control her negative thinking:

> Negative thinking has played a big part in my mental health issues. I like the term "rumination", as my dark thoughts go swirling and writhing around my head like grass in a cow's stomach, getting mashed around and looking like sludge. (Cows and other ruminants have several stomachs, and it takes a while to extract the goodness from their food.)
>
> I try to picture my black swirling thoughts being turned into something helpful, but it doesn't always work. At least I now know they are just thoughts. They can't harm

me and they are not me. I'll often try to blow them out of my mouth now, and visualise them dissipating into the air.

When I was most depressed, I think I believed in the black negative thoughts. But after lots of therapy, and with a great belief in mindfulness, I'll say "rumination, rumination" to myself and try to laugh by seeing myself as a munching cow.

Often my negative thoughts are along the lines of *I can't do this* or *I can't cope*. When that happens I try to pull myself into the present where I'm hanging out washing or cooking or something, and can do that one task if I concentrate on it.

I'd love to believe I'll never have negative thoughts again. But it's better to be realistic, and acknowledge that when they *do* come it's usually because I'm tired, harassed or overwhelmed.

It takes focus and practice to live a mindful life. But with repetition mindfulness can be an effective tool.

Another useful technique is cognitive behaviour therapy. Basically it's an understanding that thoughts come from events and feelings come from thoughts.

When we have irrational thoughts, we tend to generate feelings that are negative and hard to manage. We then behave in a way that reinforces our negative thinking. But if we challenge our irrational thoughts, the feelings we generate are much more positive.

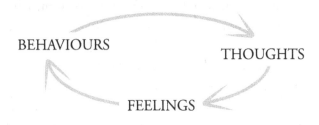

BEHAVIOURS   THOUGHTS

FEELINGS

We've talked about one type of irrational thinking—"should thinking".

Marianne, a lawyer and mum, became aware she was prone to another common type of irrational thinking—"catastrophising":

> I still have a tendency to catastrophise—overestimating the likelihood of a negative outcome, and underestimating my ability to cope if it happened. But I'm now keenly aware of the negative self-talk, and try to combat it by challenging my thoughts with more realistic ones.

She kept her negative thoughts in check by challenging them with questions such as:

- Could there be some other explanation for my thoughts?
- What evidence is there for my way of thinking?
- Is this situation really as bad as I'm making out to be?
- Is this a helpful way to think?

It's worth memorising these questions so when you recognise a negative or irrational thought you have a tool you can use to help challenge yourself.

Being a good enough parent is good enough.

I know I've already mentioned this, but it's so important I want to repeat it.

Aiming to be the perfect parent is usually a recipe for disaster. When we set ourselves goals that are impossible to achieve we're setting ourselves up for failure. There's no such thing as a perfect mum, or even a good mum. Each family is unique, and comparing one family to another is never helpful.

Sometimes women can be their own worst enemies by comparing themselves to others. Pip, who writes on this topic, accepts she's a real mum and that we're all real and vulnerable people a long way from being perfect:

> Pushing my packhorse of a pram down the street, I look like the most well-organised, in-control mum in the burbs. I have everything I need—home-cooked baby lunch in bite-sized pieces arranged in tiny containers, sippy cup, nappy bag, rain cover and sunscreen. Whatever situation may arise, Mrs In-Control can handle it.

> Completing the picture is a happy, gurgling, cheeky monkey waving at everyone from her chariot.

> But peel back the fresh concealer, peep under the fleecy duck-covered bunny rug and the reality is slightly different.

> I've probably had a hell of a night because it took two hours to settle my sweet little screaming princess. I'm aching from lack of exercise (I haven't had the time), and

no doubt smell of stale milk because I haven't had a chance to wipe down my shoulder after burping her. My mind is racing faster than a Melbourne Cup favourite, wondering what necessity I've failed to pack. And all the while I'm pondering how I'll find the time to pick up yet another bag of nappies.

So now as I pass a fellow smiling, beautiful mum on the street, I smile warmly at her and wonder what her story is. Because I now know there's a myriad of untold tales lurking behind her sunny smile and that raspberry-blowing bundle of gorgeousness.

We all have our stories. We just don't always share them.

Summary:

There's no such thing as "should".

Negative thinking can be managed with tools: mindfulness and cognitive behaviour therapy (CBT).

Being a good enough parent is good enough.

Guilt

Why do we feel so guilty when we haven't deliberately done anything wrong?

This chapter is all about guilt, and what it actually is. It will help you understand that even doing our best with the resources and knowledge we have we can still feel guilty. But when we relabel our guilt as regret, it takes away that element of blame we put on ourselves.

Mother guilt is endemic.

To feel guilty is a trademark of parenthood. To be a mum and not suffer feelings of guilt would be nothing short of a miracle.

Guilt is defined as "A feeling of responsibility or remorse for some offense, crime, wrong, etc., whether real or imagined". In the case of mums (and dads, but mostly mums), the guilt is almost always an imagined offense.

We mums can be so hard on ourselves. We sometimes blame and criticise ourselves if we achieve anything less than the unattainable standards we set for ourselves.

This sort of guilt (where we haven't actually done anything wrong) is known as "unhealthy guilt", and is often another feeling (such as anger or sadness) in disguise. When you're plagued with guilt it's worth asking yourself *What do I feel right now? What am I angry or sad about?*

Here's an example, a mum who feels guilty when she drops her two-year-old off at childcare one day a week:

> I'm at home with my child the other six days, and I'm a loving and attentive mum. But I still feel incredible guilt for going to work and having a few hours to myself.

She hasn't done anything wrong. So why does she feel so guilty? She explains:

> After much counselling I realised I was angry that my own mother worked full-time and was never there for me when I came home from school. I was mostly looked after by nannies.

This mum is angry at her own mother's absence in her past, which leads to her feeling guilty in the present. Once she became aware of her anger the guilt melted away, and she could drop her child off without feeling she was doing something wrong.

Guilt is often related our own expectations or those of our family of origin. Rigid and unrealistic expectations, such as expecting to have an immaculate home while looking after a baby, or pressure from extended families to be present when our bubs are napping, can turn on the guilt tap no end.

It's really a matter of being aware of where the guilt comes from, and being a bit easier on ourselves. We need to remember that "good enough" is a lot easier to live with than perfection.

The Supermum is a myth.

Many parents try to be everything to everyone and end up feeling guilty. It's impossible to fulfil such an all-encompassing role—something has to give or they'll burn out.

As one mum says:

> Like many others, I began motherhood far from family and old friends. Children need so many people in their lives, and in an ideal world families would be surrounded by support.

> Sometimes I wonder whether we mums know this subconsciously, and so we try to be everything and everyone to the kids. But we can't be—no parent (or parents) can be—and so we feel guilty for not being enough for them.

To me, guilt felt like a huge twanging in my heart—a huge thick elastic band being plucked. It was much worse with my first son. As I had more children I knew it would come. But I also knew I *had* to look after myself (I called it "ruthless self-care"), and I'd tell that guilt to get back in its box and leave me alone.

This mum describes guilt almost as if it has a life of its own that needs to be actively disciplined and told to contain itself—an extremely accurate analogy. If we give our guilt permission to take control, it will feed off itself and grow bigger.

Remembering that guilt is simply a passing feeling of regret, not an indication of wrongdoing, makes it lighter and easier to blow off.

Comparing yourself to others is unhelpful.

Anna is a mum who made a list of rules as a gift for her new mum friend, including this one:

> Thou shalt *never* think "everyone is coping better than I am" or feel guilty for thinking "I'm not enjoying this". Many new parents experience such emotions.

Comparing ourselves to others is like comparing apples to oranges. We all come from different families with different beliefs, resources and ideas. To think one parent does something the right and the other does it the wrong way is completely absurd.

Some of us look different to how we are feeling inside. Some of us only go to mothers' group on a good day. And some of us only open up to particular friends. These are all okay, but to assume or judge or compare won't help—ever.

We tend to judge ourselves not only on how we cope, but also on what we have (and don't have). Advertising and the media often target guilt-laden and exhausted parents wondering what they need to survive this baby phase.

One mum, Michelle, travelled thousands of kilometres to make sure she had the "right" cot for her new baby:

> When I was seven months pregnant I flew to London (from Toronto, Canada) to shop with my sister Anita. She was eight months pregnant with Daniel and had Samantha who was three, so she was the more experienced shopper. I went to be with her so we could share our pregnancies (and enormous tummies), and to shop.
>
> I needed a cot, a pram, a diaper bag, cot sheets and itsy-bitsy clothes for this baby who was growing bigger than a giant pumpkin. I seemed to have a brain block about buying these items in Toronto, which many consider a retail nirvana. I needed the support of my experienced sister, who whisked me to Brent Cross and manoeuvred me to John Lewis where we spent hours measuring and stroking cots and cribs.
>
> Two weeks later—swollen, and saturated with information from salespeople—I flew home with my flat packed purchase and special must-haves for this new baby. We spent the next few weeks erecting the beloved cot, lovingly

washing the Baby Gap linen in chambray denim, and making up this sweet space to welcome our son and heir. We hand-painted cute teddies on the wall, framed Winnie the Pooh pictures, hung mobiles, placed black and white prints at eye level—we did it all.

But baby Gabey didn't like any of it. He didn't appreciate his handmade appliqued blue and white quilt from Boba. And he didn't want to sleep in his expensive London cot that fitted exactly into the alcove of his own little bedroom.

Every time I put him in the cot, he cried. He didn't like being on his own. He just wanted to be with me, to be held and feel safe.

I listened to him. He moved into our bed, and the $700 cot was never used. It was packed up and placed behind my bedroom door.

This is a perfect example of the unnecessary pressure we put on ourselves to have the "right" stuff, and the guilt that comes with not having it.

The truth is (and always will be), there are no rights or wrongs. We're all just doing our best.

Be easy on yourself.

The good news is that as time goes by, things tend to get easier. And we also learn how to forgive ourselves for not being perfect.

One mum reminds herself that her kids have their basic needs met and that's good enough:

> *Everything* gets easier as children get older. They find friends, you make friends with other families, and some of those people become aunts and uncles to the kids.
>
> When mine started school, the guilt that once threatened to crush me finally started to lift.
>
> Like many mums who've had postnatal depression, a big part of my therapy was learning to be "good enough." I've tried taking that to heart, and some days I don't even try that hard. The kids are safe, warm and well fed. Good enough.

It's not about being the best mum, baking the best cupcakes in the best kitchen, and having the best playroom with the best toys and the most energy to play with them. No-one can sustain such a picture.

Another mum learned to be easier on herself when she thought about the past:

> The contrast of bonding from Ky to Indi was obvious. The more I connected with Indi, the guiltier I felt about Ky. I put the guilty feelings in a box and left them for another time while I got on with the job of mothering.
>
> I started forgiving myself for those first few years of disconnected mothering. I saw my son through new eyes, and we revisited those early years.

For a while he slept with me again at night. I'd hold him tight while he cried in my lap over little worries. And the more I forgave myself, the deeper our connection became.

We can always fix or improve things. So what if it doesn't happen the way we want initially? As we grow we can change and revisit. And we don't have to fix it all either.

We're all vulnerable human beings who make mistakes at times. Our children need to see we're not perfect, and that we make no apologies for this.

Summary:

Mother guilt is endemic.

The Supermum is a myth.

Comparing yourself to others is unhelpful.

Be easy on yourself.

10

How to manage unwanted advice

Short of gaffer taping their mouth shut, you can't stop people giving you unwanted advice. What you can *do is manage the way you respond to it.*

Accept that you have no control over what people say.

It's a fact of life that we can't control what comes out of a person's mouth. People will say all sorts of things, especially if they consider themselves an expert. And *many people* think they're an expert when it comes to raising children.

Anna, a chiropractor, sees a lot of new parents struggling with how to manage unwanted advice from strangers, friends and family:

> I often see confused parents after receiving unwanted advice from Aunt Sue, Bette from next door, or even a busybody at the grocery store. For the most part it comes out of genuine love and concern for their little one. But parents, especially new parents, can find much of this advice extremely overwhelming.

When you're exhausted, and climbing the steep learning curve of getting to know your baby, it's not always easy to keep your cool. After all, you know what's best for your baby. But it can be a challenge getting to this place of confidence where the comments no longer matter.

One mum was furious that her mother-in-law kept referring to her baby as "my baby":

> She'd give overbearing advice on what was best for "her baby". It's as if she claimed ownership of my child, and so knew what was best for her.

It took a lot of pain and practice to come to terms with her mother-in-law, to realise she was still the parent, and the person who was with the baby day in and day out and making all the decisions. So it didn't really matter what her mother-in-law proclaimed, judged or announced.

You do have control over how you react.

The good news is that even though you don't have control over what others say, you do have control over how you react.

One mum describes dealing with a very controlling, abusive and interfering mother:

> It's time to create my own identity and be free to be me. It's empowering, liberating and the beginning of my new life—an authentic life with the family I love.
>
> I'm not my mother, I don't need her approval, and I'm not responsible for her.

It can be challenging putting boundaries in place to help you stand firm on what advice you'll take on and what advice you'll ignore.

Brushing up on assertiveness skills is a good idea.

Using firm statements beginning with "I" is a helpful skill to practice. If a stranger asks to cuddle your baby when they're asleep in the pram, a good assertive response might be "I'm leaving the baby asleep in her pram for now". No need to justify or explain.

Often a polite nod or thank you is enough to acknowledge the advice you're given without having to justify why you're doing it differently.

One mum says:

> Follow your instinct. Opinions are like a***holes—everybody's got one.

Funny, and spot on.

It's also important to remember the people close to you can't read your mind about what you want. I often see conflict arise between a couple when one assumes the other knows what they want.

Amy discovered that what worked for her were clear messages delivered by voice (instead of telepathy):

> I found myself getting angry at my husband every night for not helping me put the kids to bed. He'd sit and read the paper as I was pulled between bedrooms patting, calming and reassuring our baby and toddler. I'm sure he would have seen steam coming from my ears, had he looked up from his newspaper.

> After months of this arrangement, it suddenly dawned on me that we hadn't ever talked about the bedtime routine. I expected him to read my mind that I resented him sitting down while I did all the work.

> After a chat I found out that he thought I enjoyed being

the Chosen One—the parent the kids preferred to connect with during the special bedtime ritual. He was happy to be invited into this part of the day.

It sounds simple, but talking actually works.

Summary:

Accept that you have no control over what people say.

You do have control over how you react.

Brushing up on assertiveness skills is a good idea.

Being a mindful parent

Mindfulness takes its roots from the Buddhist meditations thousands of years ago. It's only now being seen in the medical world as a way to manage anxiety. It even has the power to change the structure of your brain.

Mindfulness is about being present in the moment, accepting our thoughts and letting them go.

Being present with your baby is a skill.

Being mindful is about being aware. But it's more than just awareness.

We mostly use the left/logical part of our brain (a source of brooding and rumination), and ignore the right part of our brain that's responsible for intuition, thoughtfulness and creativity. But not all problems (particularly emotional ones) can be fixed with left-brain logic. Some can only be dealt with intuitively.

When we engage our intuition and creativity, we become more attuned to thoughts, emotions and sensations. We allow ourselves to be present in the moment, making full use of all our senses.

So it makes sense to apply mindfulness to our parenting. When we're mindful with our children we stop struggling to do things "the right way", stop judging ourselves, and stop trying to find answers.

Instead we use empathy and curiosity with ourselves and our kids. We see things as if we're standing in their shoes, and understand where our own reactivity is coming from. And we parent at a much deeper level—a fantastic gift for our children.

Vikki describes how she became more emotionally present while parenting her kids:

> For months I was physically present in my kids life, but not mentally. Now I'd rather have fewer hours of quality, "fully-present" time with my kids than a lifetime of not really being there at all.

Julia, a mum and GP, describes being in the moment rather than trying to get out of the moment:

> When you get frustrated, try not to wish the time away. They're only as little as they are for a short time. In no time you'll be attending your child's graduation and they'll be leaving home. The time goes so fast.

Being emotionally present with our children is how we create a connection with them.

It can be hard work to "just be" with your children. Sometimes your experience with your children and their play may feel uninspiring. And that's okay, because other times you'll find yourself smiling and enjoying just being with them.

It's important not to feel pressured to always be connected and available. As long as we're there when they need us most (when they want share a moment of joy or sadness), that's enough. No-one can be available all the time to another person—it's just setting yourself up for failure.

One mum explains how she became more focussed one moment at a time:

> Instead of talking on the phone, cooking dinner and trying to entertain the kids, I stopped and listened more. And I began to see that when you can be present with one thing, it all flows so much easier.

Another mum remembers talking to a new mum about her beliefs on bonding with her child:

I asked her to promise me, "If your baby cries, just hold him and nurture him like a mommy lion looks after her cubs. We're no different to lions, dogs or birds. It's normal and natural to listen to your baby, and support them as they grow into their bodies and learn to be safe in their own space".

This makes a lot of sense.

Connecting with you baby may be challenging.

Mums and dads react to their newborns in different ways. Not finding your baby beautiful straight away is just as normal as instantly falling in love with them. The bonding process is quick for some parents, and slow for others. And it involves many factors, including the baby's temperament, the baby's health (bonding will take longer if they're sick), and mum and dad's wellbeing.

So just remember that love might take time, and that it's perfectly okay.

A mum of three describes the challenges she overcame when bonding with her third baby:

In theatre I was given a spinal, and I reacted badly to the drugs.

So did my baby. Suddenly there was no heartbeat. The medical team cut her out quickly, but they needed to resuscitate her for nearly ten minutes.

For weeks my baby had undiagnosed reflux, and so he associated feeding (i.e. me) with pain.

It was heartbreaking. He wouldn't look at me. Newborns are supposed to look lovingly into their mother's eyes, but we had no eye contact for weeks.

This is not how it should be!

At four months of age the medication finally started, as did the bonding process. Fortunately this tenuous beginning had no effect on the loving and warm relationship we now have.

The way babies and parents form connections can vary enormously. The romanticized pictures we see on TV are rarely the reality.

And sometimes there are no extra circumstances other than fatigue that make bonding with your baby hard.

Summary:

Being present with your baby is a skill.

Being emotionally present with our children is how we create a connection with them.

Connecting with you baby may be challenging.

CHAPTER
12

Getting help

Some of us have the natural ability to ask for help. Some of us don't.

If you're in the latter group, then you may choose to practice asking for help so it becomes easier.

Remember: most people feel privileged at being asked to help.

Asking for help can sometimes be hard.

Childrearing isn't a job for one woman to do alone, even though that's exactly how it pans out for a lot of us. And many feel that asking for help is admitting defeat.

But asking for help is actually a skill that can be celebrated.

One mum said this about accepting help so you can get some rest:

> You have nothing to prove to anyone. After all, sleep deprivation has been proven as a very successful form of torture.

Another mum shares her experiences about asking for help:

> It gets easier with practice. Sometimes it's a good idea to ask people for help when you're not desperate, just to get into the habit. I do that now. And as someone who's usually more than willing to help others, I know people don't mind.

> You need a good relationship with your friends and relatives, and to trust them when they say they can help. They mean it, so don't feel guilty for asking.

It's important that you trust the person helping you. It makes the process of asking a lot easier. That's why having a support network around when there isn't a crisis is so important. It's not always easy (or even possible) to build a network during a time of need. But if it's already in place, then the soothing balm of connectedness is there for the tough times.

Help comes in many shapes and sizes.

Help may not always be asking a family member or friend for a favour or support. You may need to seek professional help, or call on alternative modalities such as meditation. Help is different for us all—we all have our own comfort zones and ideas about what is acceptable. As with anything to do with parenting, there's no right or wrong way to accept help.

One mum wrote an extensive list to remind herself what helped her. Here are some of the ways she accepted help:

Some of the things that have helped me in my journey are:

- Practical and emotional support—from friends and family who visited, made meals, cared for our daughter or took me to the doctor
- Not assuming that everyone else is coping just because they look like they're coping—many people have their own stories to tell
- Perseverance and patience
- Learning to say no—when I am feeling overwhelmed and things are getting too hard
- Learning to say yes when I need to get out of my comfort zone—it is a question of balance
- Joining a mothers' group—I made a wonderful friend through this group
- Getting out of the house with our daughter, whether it's just to the park, library or coffee shop—being with other people and in the community helps
- Talk therapy with a trusted psychiatrist and psychologist or other non-judgemental person—

sometimes it takes time to find the best one for you

- Deep breathing exercises and relaxation tapes for anxiety
- Physical exercise on a regular basis
- Making daily lists of achievable goals
- Getting out of my head by focussing on five things I can see, hear and feel
- Taking time out to do things I enjoy such as massage, shopping, movies and social activities
- Appreciating the simple things in life—hot showers, cups of tea, nice food and quiet times with family
- Minimizing time with energy draining people when I am feeling vulnerable—sometimes easier said than done
- Cognitive behavioural therapy to try and change negative patterns of thinking
- Attempting to live in the present
- Faith in God and support from church members
- Knowing the way I feel at any point in time will pass (and sometimes it changes from hour to hour)
- Limiting late nights and alcohol consumption—again it is a question of balance
- Eating well and vitamin supplements
- Having a routine or structure to my day
- Working part-time and retaining an identity outside of being a mother
- Cultivating an attitude of gratitude
- Medication
- Staying in a mother and baby unit
- Educating myself—websites such as The Smiling

> Mask and Postpartum Progress have been really helpful

This list is a brilliant reminder of just how many ways and forms help can come in.

Charles, a Melbourne GP, made up a great rule that helped him decide whether a new parent who's been to see him has received an adequate amount of help:

> There's a rule I made up called "The Sleep Rule". My friend Simon and I made it up when we were working as junior doctors in paediatrics.
>
> The Sleep Rule states that it's a doctor's job to ensure everyone sleeps well at night. That means all the work gets done during the day so people can sleep undisturbed. It means everyone who's unwell feels well enough to sleep. And it means that carers (and medical personnel) are satisfied everyone is on the path to recovery so they can sleep instead of lying awake worrying.
>
> So, if I think I'll sleep better at night by phoning a specialist or doing a test, that's all the justification I need. And I encourage parents to use the same rationale.

If you're lying awake at night unable to sleep, perhaps it's a sign your support isn't adequate and something else needs to be put in place.

Creating a community is precious.

My family attends the annual school carnival every year. It's always a great day. But although there are plenty of sweet treats, fun activities and craft stalls, they're not what makes the day so special.

What *does* make it special is the connection we all feel to the school community. It's uplifting to serve popcorn to familiar faces, be in a space where my kids feel safe and comfortable, and be a part of a group.

Connectedness has been linked to the health of individuals and community wellbeing. Being connected in the community has even been said to increase your lifespan.

One mum became well aware of this when she became a mum:

> I'm so not cut out for being alone at home with lots of children. I'm very sociable, and would be fine in an old-fashioned village where the kids run around in the mud and the mums gossip in the street and naturally help each other. A pox upon the car for changing our towns and villages so much, and making us too distant often from our neighbours.

> I wish I had family around me, but I don't. My kids need cousins, aunties, grannies and uncles around them, but they all live very far away. As parents we need to find lots of supportive and loving people for the kids, and for ourselves too.

We often use babysitters and day care and so forth in place of family support. It's not ideal, but often it's the best we can do.

It strikes me how often we don't even know our neighbours who drive into the undercover car park that leads directly indoors. And the garage door closes automatically, so there isn't even time for a wave.

In this day of automatic garage doors and dispersed extended families, it can take effort to build a community. But it's a safety net—not just for tough times, but for wellbeing.

And for always.

Summary:

Asking for help can sometimes be hard.

Help comes in many shapes and sizes.

Creating a community is precious.

Postscript: Life changes

"The only thing constant in life is change"—
François de la Rochefoucauld.

One particular day, when my second baby was only months old, I found myself pacing the floors of a local shopping centre. My baby was screaming.

There was nothing unusual about this scenario. I was used having an extremely unsettled baby. I was exhausted but this was a normal way to spend the day. However, things were starting to take their toll on me.

A lady dressed in green with a soft aura about her, appeared from nowhere. In my haze of exhaustion she breezed in front of me and almost whispered: Don't worry, it's going to be ok.

Just as quickly as she arrived, she disappeared.

She seemed to come from far away. Her Irish accent confirmed this for me. She was... other-wordly.

Normally I am not an overly spiritual person, but this lady was clearly a message to me from the pit of my exhaustion.

And she was right. It was going to be ok. Things would change.

I've moved from waking up in a cold sweat, searching for my baby among the bed sheets, to thinking about sibling rivalry, school friendships, bullying and education.

And soon my issues will be adolescence, alcohol, drugs and independence.

It took a comment from my husband one morning to get me thinking about how our routine has changed over the past few years.

We were sitting one morning reading the paper when my husband said he'd read the paper from cover to cover and needed something else to read. I too had just about tackled everything in the Sunday paper of interest to me.

So why is this something to write home about? Because having time to myself *at home* with my four- and seven-year-old also in the house is something that's taken a bit of time to arrive at.

Progress is so slow that I almost forgot what it used to be like. Just a few years back our Sunday morning routine was being woken by a baby at 5am, and then leaving by 7am for a rushed walk and coffee to make it home for baby's 8am nap.

I'm grateful for slower Sunday mornings, and the growing independence of my kids. At the time it seemed the exhaustion and early rising would never end. But it did, and our parenting joys and challenges moved forward to the next stage.

And so will yours.

Recommended further reading

The Dad Factor by Richard Fletcher
This book provides information for dads on becoming a parent. It's written by a psychologist from Newcastle who is well regarded in this area of research in Australia.

Rekindling your Relationship by Martien Snellen
This book will provide tools to help you with your relationship once baby has come along. Written by a Melbourne Psychiatrist who works in a mother baby unit.

Towards Parenthood by J. Milgrom, J. Erickson, B. Leigh, Y. Romeo, E. Loughlin, R. McCarthy and B. Saunders
Preparing for the changes and challenges of a new baby—very similar to issues discussed in this book.

Becoming Us by Elly Taylor
Written by a counsellor based in Sydney.

Becoming Us highlights key opportunities for growth and connection, and tackles the most common relationship challenges such as expectations, intimacy and conflict. It provides practical and insightful approaches to resolving tricky issues and deepening your relationship at the same time.

Through loving, learning and growing together, we can find just how much it's possible to gain from sharing the parenting experience.

Motherguilt by Ita Buttrose and Dr Penny Adams
Australian women reveal their true feelings about motherhood—a truly reassuring read that we are all very similar.

The MotherDance—How Children Change Your Life by Harriet Lerner
Lerner shows us how kids are the best teachers of life's most profound spiritual lessons.

Parenting from the Inside Out by Daniel J. Siegal and Mary Hartzell
Being a self-aware and mindful parent, and connecting with your children.

Beyond The Baby Blues by Catherine Knox, Benison O'Reilly and Seana Smith
The complete perinatal depression and anxiety handbook.

Other recommended resources

PANDA—Post and Antenatal Depression Association
Ph: 1300 726 306
www.panda.org.au

Pregnancy, Birth and Baby Helpline
Ph: 1800 882 436

Suicide Line
Ph: 1300 651 251
www.suicideline.org.au

Lifeline
Ph: 131114
www.lifeline.org.au

Mensline
Ph: 1300 78 99 78
www.menslineaus.org.au

Beyond Blue
Ph: 1300 224 636
www.beyondblue.org.au

Acknowledgements

Thank you to the amazing people who contributed to (and believed in) this book:

Bill Harper, Lael Stone, Dr Charles Alpren, Danny Blaker, Marianne Bastiani, Renee Kam, Sarah Wilson, Michelle Wright, Paul Benveniste, Rachel Rugers, Dr Julia Driscoll, Joanne Kosylo, Annette Marlow, Michelle Coxhead, Elly Taylor, Pip McDonald, Vikki Friedman, Seana Smith, Anna Beaton, Lisa Young, Amy Thompson, Anna Kula, Pinky McKay, Dr Sam Margis, Neroli Marke-Hutton, Dr Deirdre Percy and Barry Ridout.

And thanks to the many other women and men who contributed but wish to remain anonymous.

Reviews

All the frozen casseroles in the world can't prepare you for the emotional roller coaster that comes with a new baby. However, Dr Melanie Strang can guide you through this maze of "mother feelings" with empathy, understanding and simple practical strategies. *Mother Love* should be on every new mother's coffee table, for reassurance that she is not alone, that she is a "good enough" mother and, with the right support, she can enjoy this precious and exciting time with confidence.

Pinky McKay (Lactation Consultant and Baby Care Author)

What an important topic to cover…of course there are many "cookbooks" telling parents how to parent, but not enough helping parents feel good about their parenting. Dr Strang is to be applauded for tackling this crucial transition and the emotional "strollercoaster" that it is for so many.

Dr. Sam Margis, Consultant Perinatal Psychiatrist, NEST family wellness clinic

Dr Melanie Strang's book is a raw and earthy way of drawing parents' real life experiences together. Melanie in her book has collectively drawn these stories together in a very intimate and personal manner. She delivers a common sense approach in drawing upon parent's own stories to offer a solution of personal growth in a positive light as to what new parents are feeling and adjusting to parenthood.

As a midwife and childbirth educator I feel it is my role to give expectant parents a glimpse into how this can impact upon their lives. Melanie's book offers insight for new and expectant parents on the dilemmas that they may face. The book explores the not so idealistic, romantic perceptions and media build up to parenthood and encourages parents to seek support during this time.

Neroli Marke-Hutton, Midwife and Childbirth Educator

I really like the book, it covers many of the things I try to pass on to patients while pregnant or in the first few months, that I learnt along the way either with my own kids or while nannying. I think it will be very helpful to anyone starting out parenting, to get their expectations in a more realistic and kinder space.

I love the short simple format and bullet point summaries—just right for a new parent's attention span!

I would certainly recommend it to my patients to read and we will look forward to having a copy in the waiting room.

What a great achievement to get it all down on paper. It reads easily but I know concise and clear writing is an art! Well done!
Dr Deirdre Percy, Obstetrician, Orrong Obstetrics and Gynaecology